D1168428

# Scavenger
# LOOP

# Scavenger
# LOOP

POEMS

DAVID BAKER

W. W. NORTON & COMPANY
NEW YORK  LONDON

For information about permission to reproduce selections from this book,
write to Permissions, W. W. Norton & Company, Inc.,
500 Fifth Avenue, New York, NY 10110

For information about special discounts for bulk purchases, please contact
W. W. Norton Special Sales at specialsales@wwnorton.com or 800-233-4830

Manufacturing by Courier Westford
Production manager: Julia Druskin

Library of Congress Cataloging-in-Publication Data

Baker, David, 1954–
[Poems. Selections]
Scavenger loop : poems / David Baker. — First edition.
pages ; cm
ISBN 978-0-393-24612-4 (hardcover)
I. Title.
PS3552.A4116A6 2015
811'.54—dc23
                                        2015000687

W. W. Norton & Company, Inc.
500 Fifth Avenue, New York, N.Y. 10110
www.wwnorton.com

W. W. Norton & Company Ltd.
Castle House, 75/76 Wells Street, London W1T 3QT

1 2 3 4 5 6 7 8 9 0

*for Stanley Plumly*

# CONTENTS

# ACKNOWLEDGMENTS

These poems first appeared in the following periodicals, to whose editors I extend my grateful acknowledgment: *The Account*, "Two Iguanas," "What You Said"; *The American Poetry Review*, "On Arrogance," "What Is a Weed?"; *At Length*, "Scavenger Loop"; *The Atlantic Monthly*, "Heaven"; *The Chronicle of Higher Education*, "Swift"; *FIELD*, "Corner Window," "Our Ivy"; *Five Points*, "The Quiet Side Street (1)"; *New England Review*, "Simile"; *The New Republic*, "Hamartia"; *Northwest Review*, "Who Knew"; *Plume*, "Errand," "Flood," "Of Shine"; *Poem-a-Day* (Academy of American Poets), "As a Portent," "Belong To"; *Poetry*, "Metastasis"; *Raritan*, "The Windmill"; *Shenandoah*, "Twelve Bells"; *The Southern Review*, "Outside"; *The Southwest Review*, "Magnolia"; *Virginia Quarterly Review*, "The Anniversary," "Five Odes on Absence," "The Quiet Side Street (2)"; *The Yale Review*, "Fall Back."

I am grateful also to Denison University for support and encouragement and to Jill Bialosky for the gift of her guidance.

# ONE

# Swift

### 1.

into flight, the name as velocity,
a swift is one of two or three hundred
swirling over the post office smokestack.
First they rise come dusk to the high sky,

flying from the ivy walls of the bank
a few at a time, up from graveyard oaks
and backyards, then more, tightening to orbit
in a block-wide whirl above the village.

### 2.

Now they are a flock. Now we're holding hands.
We're talking in whispers to our kind, who
stroll in couples from the ice cream shop
or bike here in small groups to see the birds.

A voice in awe turns inward; as looking
down into a canyon, the self grows small.
The smaller swifts are larger for their singing,
the spatter and shrill, the high *cheep* of it.

### 3.

And their quick bat-like alternating wings.
And the soft pewter sky sets off the black
checkmark bodies of the birds as they skitter
like water toward a drain. Now one veers,

dives, as if wing-shot or worse out of the sky
over the maw of the chimney. Flailing—
but then pulling out, as another dips
and the flock reverses its circling.

4.

They seem like leaves spinning in a storm,
blown wild around us, and we are their witness.
Witness the way they finish. The first one
simply drops into the flue. Then four,

five, in as many seconds, pulling out of
the swirl, sweep down. So swiftly, we're alone.
The sky is clear of everything but night.
We are standing, at a loss, within it.

# On Arrogance

I thought I
killed it—too
    little water. Too much sunlight.
    Wrong pot: bad plan: what-

ever. So
says my girl, when it's all too much
    to deal with. A
    difficult thing's easier

to dismiss these
days than
    face. I know. I hung
    three ferns on the porch so she would

find it homey, like home had been,
and I would too.
    Who knew
    the robins started there in stealth?

By the time
I saw their nest the fern
    was sickly gray, a
    maw in the middle of fronds

splayed like shocked hair.
Twice I poured

my spout of water beneath
the nest; got buzzed, cussed, harped at

from the power line running
from the porch.
    Whatever. I let them go, and they were born.
    I hoisted neighbor kids for

a look—tiny brown
puddle of bodies in a cup,
    bubble eyes, splayed beaks, such
    rapt new hunger—

but not Kate: not
interested. I took
    photos to show. Not Kate.
    They grew, and then—one on a Tuesday,

the next two
the next day—they flew.
    I hear her calling across long
    shadows of green yards

some days, or think
I do. Today
    it was the cat
    at the screen door, yowling to get back in—

and him with a mouthful
of bird. Good boy.

He dropped it at my feet
and stood there

unblinking upward, wanting
his simple scratch, and all I could think
    was Jesus, David, now
    what have you done?

# Simile

1.

Orange-and-midnight the moth on the fringe tree—
first it nags a bloom; sips and chews; then shakes
the big flower. Then its wings slow. Grows
satiate, as in sex. Then still, as the good sleep after.
Each bloom a white torch more than a tree's flower.
Each is one of ten or twelve, conic, one of many
made of many green-white or white petals
held out, as by a hand, from the reach of the limb.
A field this morning was full of white moths. More
in the side yard, in the bluebottle, lifting—fog
off the dew, white wings like paper over flames
and floating awry or pieces of petal torn off.
Weeks now my words on paper have burned.
Burned and flown, like a soul on fire, with
nothing to show but ash, and the ash flies too.


2.

Today, in the news—so many martyrs—
an "unnamed suicide bomber" took herself into
the arms of flame, and five others, "by her own hand."
Whitman means the beauty of the mind is terror.
*Do you think I could walk pleasantly and*
*well-suited toward annihilation?*
But there is no likeness beyond her body
in flames, for its moment, no matter its moment.
Yet the fringe bloom burns. Yet the moth shakes
and chews, as in sex. When the young maple

grows covered with seeds, they are a thousand
green wings, like chain upon chain of keys,
each with its tiny spark, trying the black lock.
A tumbler turns and clicks. The world once more
fills with fire, and the body, like ash, is ash.

# Fall Back

A golden rainfall

there is no rain

and it brushing side-

long and windless

three sugar maples

turning their leaves

out in a shower

of sun and the dew

that all this night

settled heavy there

blazing off so quickly

the lightening leaves

quiver like mirrors

over the miniature

crab apple its

thousand fruits

the birds don't touch

and late season

green tomatoes shining

        in a hoar of frost—

what have we done

        with this chance this day

but turn our backs as

        leaves turn to light

over two blue chairs we

        painted years ago, nails

working out of those

        weathered arms

what have we done

        but slept through it—

# What Is a Weed?

1.

Emerald, as in the leaf of the ash,
though nothing's burned, not yet, as the ash-green,
gray-green fiery wingspan of the adult
whose bullet body and "flat black eyes" are
less the way we know them than by the trees,
by the death of the trees, by the millions.
The adults emerge, *A. planipennis*
(of the genus *Agrilus*), in May, June,
July, then in bark crevices, between
layers of the diamond derma, females
set their eggs whose larvae, in a week, bore
back into the trees. They chew the phloem.
They eat the inner body of the bark,
creating winding galleries as they feed.
This "cuts the flow" of water nutrients
to the tree. This "causes dieback," causes death.

2.

What is a weed? What I saw was a tree.
A thousand trees in the village, more, but
one at the point of the street corner lot
where all summer I held my girl by the back
of her bike and ran the green block down.
The tree was obvious, catalpa, its long
three-branching trunks splayed like a birch, whose
shagbark white parchment skin is equally

unmistakable—leaves as big as a
piece of paper, if the page were a heart
or head of a spade, and pale green, foot-long-at-
least bean pods dangling like ropy toys—
three trunks pushing from our one earth, equally
thick, the same height. And then, between two trunks
of waving catalpa, I saw ash leaves, fist-
sized but delicate, blooming from the third.

3.
All over the village the ashes are
dying. Already dead, my tree friend says.
The scourge emerald borer rode in on
shipping crates, Asia via Lake Erie,
2002. They date it to the month.
And in bundles of firewood, in luggage
of travelers, in bedding plants, their radiant
splay spread "like wildfire," up Ontario,
down, through Ohio, Illinois . . . and now
7.5 billion ash trees, mountain
white (*Fraxinus americana*) and blue,
fragrant, Carolina, green, (family of
Oleaceae), of opposite branching,
of compound pinnate leaf, whose timber is
"wonderfully springy," excellent for oars
and tools, "and lends itself to steaming and

4.

turning," as in bentwood furniture, will die.
Though some refer to them as trash. Trash ash.
What is a weed? And the answerer says
a plant that doesn't fit the local plan.
In my personal doctrine of signatures
you can tell the emerald ash borer
simply by its hole, the letter D, as
it emerges from the host—each circle
with its flattened edge or side—a hundred
or more, like buckshot, on a tree sometimes,
or on a tree braided to another tree.
Two catalpas growing with a third.
I pushed my daughter down the street, let go,
and her laughter lit the waiting trees—ash
or trash, catalpa, oak . . . the neighborhood
where she learned to fly. Then the trees grew wings.

# Magnolia

We were done for. Things broken. Things ugly.
　It being the shut end of night. Morning breaking, more
like a bruise smeared through the wet few uppermost leaves.
Not yet light so much as less dark. They shouldn't grow
this far north. That's what the book says. What book.
　What I meant was, each day begins in the dark.
That's useless that's too late that's a pathetic thing to say—
　older than bees the magnolia. More primitive, the book
says, whose carpels are extremely tough. They do not flower
in sepals. They do not want such differentiation
in their flower parts, from whence the term tepals.
　They open, the anthers, splitting themselves out. That's your
melodrama. No they split at the front facing the flower center.
　16-something. Pierre Magnol. Morning starting through them
like a purple bruise, then a cloud, as one small pale blue
　stretchmark, another, then another. That's not right.
Flowers developed to encourage pollination by beetles. Too
　early for bees. Grew tough to avoid damage by said beetles.
—There you have it. *Magnolia virginiana*. Subfamily
　Magnolioideae of the family Magnoliaceae.
Relations have been puzzling taxonomists for a long time—
　to survive ice ages, tectonic uptearing, slow drift
of the continents, a distribution scattered. Things too old
　for change, mutinous in the half-light, and malignant.
Stop it please please. They shouldn't be this far north.
　They bloom in a cup of pink fire, each one, lit by an old oil.
Before us the bees. Before us the bees the beetles. These trees
　—so what. We had walked out earlier, the porch, late

terrible dark night. Their natural range a disjunct dispersal.
No light. The magnolia. The eye begins to see. Then the long
horrible scrape on its trunk, his single stretching paring
of the bark back. But he didn't finish his discomfort, his
antler velvet a cloud of sawdust and scrapings beneath like
small remains of a cold fire. All night trying, then no
longer trying, that's when we walked out. He must have run.

# Five Odes on Absence

1.

> *M Drst,* he starts, *M nrl wrn t* . . .

And if purple's the new black as *Vogue* says
(according to their latest ad-by-tweet,
*it s the seasons thing*), perhaps erasure's
our poetry du jour. At the Walker
contemporary poets have been
composing "astounding new work" by
removing portions of existing . . .

> *Nbd wll wn M r hv m* . . . *& wht hv dn* . . .

"Join us as several guest poets read from
and display their latest or landmark e-
rasures." Which means: take Dickinson, rub
some letters out, you can be famous, too.
Because I could not stop for Death—make that
Be a cold sop. I stood at—. You get the
picture. Sappho: without time's injury.

> *ppl tll m hv gt n hm n ths wrld* . . .

2.

My neighbor's boy Bernard is practicing.
*Bang* against his father's garage, painted
a week ago, taupe siding and light brown
sliding doors trimmed out and edged in white.

*Bang* and three dozen grackles scatter off
the ornamental crab where they had lit.
Beautiful tree to be so full of birds.
Beautiful birds whose shape maintains a tree

when they disperse, silhouette widening
like a flower blooms, or limbs in blue flight.
*Bang* and his skates scrape down the concrete drive.
He taps his stick—he digs his rollers in—

Bernard's usually dead-eyed with a puck
but wild today. *Thwack*. Paint puff. One more scar
on the door where he's missed the net once more.
That's his father watching from the window.

That's his mother not there, not there, not there—

3.
Mr. Clare wants a little privacy.
Who can blame him? It's 1849.
All his life he's tried to get the words right—
           *hurried*
*The startld stockdove* ~~wizzing~~ *bye*
                    *the sky*
*As the still hawk hangs oer* ~~him~~ *in dusk*
                              *as they*
*Crows from the oaks trees qawking* ~~flush~~ *spring*
~~Wafting the stillness of the woods~~ —


get the birds right. Get the trees. It's not code
exactly. Now he's the talkative in-
mate/patient of Northampton County
General Lunatic Asylum; and
now he's boxed with gipsies, written *Don
Juan*, lived on grass one mad escape home
*and yet thou art not there.* And now he writes


to Mary Collingwood (is she Mary
Bolland? is she Patty?) *Drst Mr
r fthfll r d thnk f m* . . . pulling
out the vowels, *dd vst me n hll,*
leaving out the *y*'s, *sm tm bck . . . flsh
ppl tll m hv gt n hm n ths wrld . . .*
Who can blame him? He gets confused,

*hope*

weaving it this way. *Is faded all ~~a thought~~.*
He lived in a house with seven children,
*whr r th* . . . He was the rage of London,
peasant poet, friend of . . . *whr r th* . . .
Some days now he pulls weeds to keep busy,
though his doctors want him inside, enclosed
for safety's sake. He sings them little songs.

*I am—yet what I am, none cares or knows;*
*My friends forsake me like a memory lost:*
*I am the self-consumer of my woes.*
3,000-plus poems in a lifetime,
not code exactly, not exactly not.
*bt dnt cm hr gn fr t s*
*ntrs bd plc . . . rs fr vr & vr*
*                    Jhn Clr*

4.
Morandi paints a bottle by painting
everything around the bottle but not
the bottle. This is how it always is.
Wherever I am I am what is missing.
*Twiteren*: birdsong; tremble; high-pitched laughter;
state of great agitation; quiver; ~~eye~~
*I feel I am—I only know I am*
*And plod upon the earth as dull and void:*
The keyword is verisimilitude.
It's not enough to tell the truth; you have
to tell it in believable fashion.
Then buyers won't care what you omit—
*Earth's prison chilled my body with its dram*
*Of dullness and my soaring thoughts destroyed.*
Tweeting is writing messages of
140 characters or less,
no matter the message, using @Twitter.
These are live updates of what one's doing.
*I fled to solitudes from passion's dream.*
*But now I only know I am—that's all.*

5.
Some days Isaac sits on the deck all day.
He holds his head. He drinks a lot. He weeps.
The birds are landing black, then purple, as
the sun picks up the oils on their wings.
The heavy crab grows heavier with them.
The pink blossoms grow shivery, like wings.
I understand the patience. Sometimes I do.

I wonder what Bernard sees when he sees
the open net yawning there. Toward the end
Morandi painted fewer lines—bigger
ghosts. Made an edge with a sketch of edges
behind the pale line of each edge. That's all
it takes, innuendo of a thing, the way,
*bang*, now the grackles explode out again

in a crazy puff of wings. Bernard's rage
is the hard pink downfall of petals there,
or not there, as he skates back down the drive.
I sit with my magazines and cell phone.
I feel crazy drifting by myself.
Sometimes I think the birds are shadows of
some other thing—I just can't see it well—

black, then purple, then purple turning black.
You get the picture. On a better day

Clare writes, the starnels darken down the sky.
But that's the price of time's erasure, too,
sad memories of a happier life.
*Ppl mk sch mstks.* It isn't code . . .
*whr r* . . . Then what he doesn't write is you.

# Belong To

See the pair of us

*Raining and morning*

*the first soft ashes*

along the high road

running the far ridge

of pines ripped wild to

timbers by storming

to shreds see the white

shreds *like coals* like a

sudden sorrow see

the partial moon see

the cut sky see us

serene with singing

are we merry are

we rueful neither

is there sufficient

wording for what falls

*all the muffled horns*

pleading but too late

                    along the last route

of what remains can

                    you see us what can

you see there—*lost leaves*

                    *waiting to come back*

*as leaves—*

# TWO

# Errand

The fawn was
born beneath the hydrangea I had mistaken,
    for a year, as a young oak.

I squatted there. No
fear. It lay alone
    in the leaves, and at my near touch a tuft

of its skin (you couldn't
call it
    hide, barely fur, still birth-

smeared in smatters
of pale gray spots)—
    one tuft of skin quivered, as

though cold.
Even this first day
    the doe had gone to find herself

something to eat
in a better yard. Error on
    error, a life amasses.

Do you believe
the old poet—not
    to be born is reckoned best

of all?
So let's ask
        the bird dog gagging at his chain

two yards over, bloody with boredom.
Ask the night-
        black vultures, kettling

over the neighbor's burn pile.
I had somewhere
        to go. I don't know where, but

how could it
matter, so much, to go?
        Smell of snow an hour

before it falls,
then doesn't. Soft leather
        nose of the fawn, wet in my palm

where it nestled its warm
jaw in. To make
        a cathedral (I should have stayed) of such things . . .

# The Windmill

First the *tsk* of the

trowel then a glint

like a rusty tooth

I was dividing

hostas from fiddle

head ferns musk of pine-

resin asphalt waves

brewing in the new

development beyond

in a few seconds

I had unearthed

the whole rotor twelve

blunt blades where it was

buried or collapsed

who knows why

when wind turned my head

to hear from a

window a child's voice

cry out *no more!*—

                               at which instant

the green heron pulled away from the pond—

# Flood

Immensity of song—to be so small
that throat—
that singer     wren on a red
tree—
amid the wicks of wet fruit.
*And a light comes up*
in and out of the houses
I hung there.
In and out,
of climbing hydrangea,


each house-hole *trumpeting*
*like loud flowers*
the size of a quarter—
all week, flitting
through hanging ferns, cocked tail,
blunt chest. What big
song.
And the little birds,
brown as buns,
in and around the trees—


You want to keep a lot
of water out
*what?*—is what he said.
Yes of course. All
I could think was wings,

*but that's not*
        *true.* But partly
also this, the end of it, what we'd been,
        rain in
the night not rain but sheets,


        wild, torrents
claiming every dry thing until
        buckled there the very under-
pinning of the house. Yes
        faster than the pumps.
Easy, he said, block
        auger—*weep-holes* is what he said—
backhoe   pickaxe   you want to keep a lot of water
        out   *bright song*   let
a little in—

# Outside

                    Stevie lives in a silo.
A silo lives where, mostly, Stevie is
or is not. Tipped over—a hollow vein.
The silo, I mean. For here home is out
there on the grass. If you want a drink or wash
your hands, just dip into that trunk, hot and cold
running branches feeding down. It's startling.
But sense is startling, too. See how those boots
flip skyward? Tongues lapping up dew on his
mache dandelions. This is Stevie's dream

mini-acreage on the family's old spread.
He's all spread out. He's humming when he makes
a working thing—he won't let you inside.
So, he says. Today he's stacked two propane
tanks and ovens—two-burners—under a
red maple and when you open a door
there's mismatched silver and hatchets and things
he's made to eat *and* art with. Studio
as wherever-you're-itching-at-the-time:
boards with big nails banged in and from the nails

hang gourds, baby-sized cups spackled yellow
(is that old egg?), a hundred kinds of who
knows what, the center being where you are
and are not. I stay dry, he says. No bugs.
Says why do walls want windows? He's put glass
around his trees instead, head-high to look

at trees from outside out. One chair, sleeping bag
—what he keeps inside his wild corn bin—
plus a getaway, by which he means a tunnel.
Oh oh, he says, they coming. He can worm

his way all the way to the apple trees.
He trenched it out last fall and lights the route
with flashlights and tinfoil clipped to clothesline.
That's a trip. And that's a curvy planter full
of nursery nipples and hand-dipped Ken dolls.
If you want to see one art made wholly
in an outside mind, come see Stevie's crib.
That's his ten-foot pink polyvinyl penis
teeter-totter beside the birdcage
for tomatoes. Take a ride, he says. All eyes.

# Who Knew

1.
it takes
(his reply) as long as
    it takes.

    Now we know.
Blue sky like plate-
glass

etched with branchings there,
aftermath wind
    as broad as
    it is long,
and the red maple cracked
straight through

standing still upright.
So when the tree man's
    front tire
    broke the soft
earth at least
he didn't fall—got

his bucket
cranked down;
    got centered; got himself un-
    buckled
to hop off the
high backside in time (*something's up there—in*

*the trees*—), his truck
stuck like a kicked-up root
    where the hole opened below.
    Why the *hell*
didn't you
(his emphasis) *tell* me?


2.
Who knew?
Fifteen feet off the corner
    of the barn
    (*that's a*
*carriage house*—)
a century-old


cistern, granite-lined, intact,
and once more
    darker-in-daylight
    where planks and a
cover of sod
gave way to the truck's weight


yawned again.
We shoved, we spun,
    we pushed the fenders, and
    then he was gone.
But now ghosts
of deer and possum, feral

cats, voles, the smaller field mice (*who knows
what*) come
     to crouch
     beside the blackened
pool each night,
all week, stone

and starlight
where the water was. Let them
     drink deeply here,
     shadows-among-shadows,
who wait for us under
falling trees.

# Corner Window

So quiet I hear

          the streetlight ticking

red recycling back

          to yellow then red

we know the depth of

          things by what they're not

how empty the sky

          how vast    the few stars

as in emphasis

     •

          the ones I love are

far away one is

          hurting she cannot

talk who wears a mask

          to help her breathe

when I spoke her name

          tonight by cell phone

trying to be happy

          what did she hear

•

rain coming before

        it rains a low wind

seething in the trees

        far off then nearer

under my lungs that

        same sweep adrenal

is small relief that dread

        like dread lifting

or like a little

        bit of happiness

is grief   growing darker—

# Twelve Bells

Each day
was a day

like every
other one.

She had gone
without

word or
scant sign.

Meals came,
were done.

High clouds
spun in

the white
ethers.

Daily busi-
ness ran,

still poorly,
and was

concluded
by phone

or in the
fine print

of the evening
tribune.

Then the bells
chimed one

noontide,
like a gun.

He recalled
the only

news worse
than none,

in that
region, was

still delivered
by hand.

## As a Portent

At least there was a

                song    timorous of

wingbeat snowdrift ash

                of red horizon

then somewhere calling

                *as under one's breath*

(I did not hope you

                would find me wanting)

and the next extinction

                on every wing—

# THREE

# Scavenger Loop

*Buddy, can I dig?*
But he's already
   deep into it, pile I've dragged
   all morning, piece by piece, to the curb.

He's a seasoned picker
—I can tell—his CRV backed up
   right to the rubble and
   hatchback popped open, half-full, at 9 a.m., of

whatnots and what-ifs: heirloom
silver in a hand-tooled box, a baby's clothes, books
   in bright wrappers.
   He's come from a county away

to score—his term—whatever he can
the day before
   our village "free-for-haul"
   is officially underway.

*In the wild, animals lie where they die, thus placing them into the scavenger loop. The upshot is that the highly concentrated animal nutrients get spread over the land, by the exodus of flies, beetles, etc.*

•

You need to get home as soon as you can.
The doctor thinks you should come back, *right now—*

•

*Dustscaewung* . . . a kind of daydream of dust, a pondering of that which has been lost: dust-*seeing*, dust-*chewing*, dust-*cheering*. The daydream of a mind strung between past and present.

Row on row of rich green stalks.

•

Something is coming more than we know how.

An hour ago on Facebook one newly
friended friend posted: Repeal Monsanto
Protection Act, as it "deregulates
the GMO industry from any
court oversight." This status update was
"shared" from a status update which picked it
from someone else's status, and so on.
Seventy-seven people "like" this post—
a record for me, my new friend comments
in the comment box of her own update.
*A complex and mobile intimacy* . . .

                    •

as in old woods,            as when a single tree
dies, and starts to rot,    yet it may remain
for decades. "More than     a third of the bird
species depend on           standing dead trees,
both for their food and     for nesting places."
The body decays and         the larvae of some
"specialist beetles"        process the wood for
tiny tastes of nu-          tritious starch inside—
their burrows, maybe        only "one to three
millimeters wide,"          spill a powdery
sawdust as they chew:       *powderpost, deathwatch,*
*tinder polypore,*          *sulfur shelf, sapsucker*—.
The wood returns to         the soil as humus.

The road out of town . . .
    and always the same road
back—

*The USDA projected 2013 US corn production at 14,140 million
bus, based on the Prospective Plantings number of 97.3 million acres
planted, 8% average abandonment resulting in harvested area of
89.5 million acres, and an average yield of 158 bus an acre.*

·

I am her son    *sign here*    She's my mother

·

*I am up to a hundred "likes" OMG*

·

Apologizes to the doctor    that she's dying—

Cessation of the furosemide *loop
diuretic*, cessation of O$_2$—

                    •

That's a pacemaker not a defib who—

                    •

She sang "Yellow Bird" when she was happy—

                    •

1 farmer :: 151 consumers
farm and ranch families < 2%
of the national population—

                    •

Her mysteries her bells her soaps her coats—

                    •

Didn't this used to be Johnny's Sinclair?—

                    •

When I asked what she needed—water—soup—
she said *7UP     tiramisu!*—

                    •

*When we reduce biodiversity by breaking up the forest for our
backyards, we accidentally free undiluted disease organism{s}
to operate at full strength . . .*

                    •

*You may not be tired but I'm tired—*

•

Night sky so vast    hear the wheat roar—

SmartStax RIB Complete, a single bag refuge
solution against earworm, army worm.

Row on hundreds of rows of rich green stalks—
*knee high by the 4th of July* and eight

feet or more before the fall—Monsanto
"offers corn farmers the ability

to control weeds and pests with a single
seed through a process known as 'trait stacking.'"

Thus DroughtGard Hybrids, VT Triple PRO
for aboveground insect protection stacked with

belowground rootworm protection and Round-
up Ready 2 Technology to fight

Goss's Wilt, Gray Leaf Spot, chronic drought, corn
borer . . .

      •

                        rummaging each other's trash heaps—

      •

*We deny that we are animals and part of the wheel of life, part
of the food chain. We deny that we are part of the feast and
seek to remove ourselves from it, even though we kill and
consume animals by the billions and permanently remove the
life resources for many more. But not one animal is allowed to
consume us, even after we are dead. Not even the worms.*

*Give him some money    Is it muddy there*

*        is it    Four up five up six up seven*

*up seven up    Can we go now    I want*

*        to go now please    David some money    Please*

*is it nice is it muddy is it some*

*        money    Sweet the    Hmm    Hmm    Let's go today*

*I want to go    Tomorrow    Sun    Today*

*        What can you see already from the chair*

*Is it    Bubbles I like them    Must can we go*

*        Hmm    Eight up nine up eleven twelve—*

*David Philip Dayle David Philip Dayle*

*        those are my men    What can you see now*

*oh grace the Come on    Come now    Oh no my*

*        is it muddy honey awful I'm not—*

*I'm just a picker*, he says.
It's a hobby, not subsistence. *Leastways not*
    *hereabouts.* Treasure hunter,
    geocacher, scrounge . . .


    •


*skawage*, Middle English :: customs—as from

*escauwage*, Old North French :: inspection—as from

*scēawian*, Old English :: to look at—or lately

with some "semantic drift," English :: show—


    •


decomposers and detritivores complete the process by consuming
remains left by scavengers—

She was fifteen
maybe, riding her bike those long evenings
down old AA where it all turned blacktop
and gravel past the Lindsey place farther
than the quarry pool. Evening fireflies
above the soybeans. Swallows in the air.
She was never in a hurry. Once in

a little sprinkle she pulled off the road
and we saw slung over her back wheel like
saddlebags a cluster of plastic milk-
cartons she used riding around to tweak
her product. A week later her huffer-
chef-boyfriend blew up their stove and him with it.
She didn't die though her forehead melted

and a few fingers fighting it off and
her hair, part of one ear, top lip, you know,
lucky girl. Row on row by the thousands
of tall stalks growing so straight they seem combed,
every twenty rows a seed sign to mark
varietals of the labs' latest tests,
Agrigold 6267 Agrigold 6472 . . .

Peck baskets line the

              market sidewalk packed

with local apples

              the sheriff's running

more folks off for

              loitering so the streets

are quiet nights

              so much depends

on what they

              tell you for your

patronage or vote

              so much more

as malathion

              in the skin on what

they don't—

•

*Come, kill the Worm, that doth its kirnell eate*
*And strike thy sparkes within my tinderbox.*

•

An average of nine different fungicides and pesticides
discovered in bee pollen are tied to Colony Collapse Disorder—

•

Who would I show it   *so unprocessed* to—

Her letter, started years ago, leaving
*Evelyn's pie safe. Waterford bells.*


*Grandmother's thimbles her material.*
How do you keep a thing you cannot touch?


Agrigold 6376.
*Portrait of the boys above the table.*


Denbeigh Acres Our Manors Have Manners.
Four names. One crossed out. Heirlooms edited.


*Quilts towels Mother hand-stitched some linens*
*pillowcases* [     ] FOPs tolerant.


Walk around and stick a yellow Post-it
on the stuff you want is what he told me.


Nutcracker Kitchen—cornbread from heaven.
*14 China Birds.* Publix Cineplex.


International Harvester. Archer
Daniels Midland, Tyson, ConAgra, Swift . . .

The world gives you itself in fragments / in splinters:

•

*The grey lawns cold where gold, where quickgold lies!*
*Wind-beat whitebeam! airy abeles set on a flare!*
*Flake-doves sent floating forth at a farmyard scare!*
*Ah well! it is all a purchase, all is a prize.*

•

['splɪn tər]

•

*n.*

a very small sharp piece of wood, glass, metal, etc., characteristically
long and thin

broken off from the main body;

(Military, Firearms, Gunnery, Ordnance & Artillery) a metal fragment,
from the container of a shell, bomb, etc., thrown out during explosion;

splinter group, separate factions, sect; as of church, as of family;

*obs.* secured by splint or splints—

*vb.*
to reduce or be reduced to sharp fragments;

shatter;

break off in small shards—

Tell me, where does it hurt? *Everywhere else—*

—broken shutters, musty box
springs, two ancient-at-
    eight-years-old laser printers
    and all manner of lawnmowers, power tools, hand

tools, shredded planters, to name only a bit
of the stuff crammed
    in my barn: as for me,
    fewer loves, yet more

amassed . . . as there, out
behind the barn, the pile of waterlogged lumber
    where the new fawns
    this spring were born, and farther yet, between

oak leaf hydrangeas and scrub trees
I've thinned out
    for cosmetic sake, for fewer leaves to rake,
    for more sun, thick grass (thus

the complexity of the whole
system diminished:
    another *positive feedback loop* lost)—
    there, beyond

the village's big houses,
there, past nail parlors,
    the franchise hardware shop, fast-food shacks
    and tattoo sheds,

beyond the strips, the burbs,
there, the sunken barns
    where row on row
        the fields spread, running out through the country,

the corn fields, the soy beans,
for ten miles, a hundred
    more, for
        a thousand miles of *rich green stalks* . . .

Removal of IV    pulse 16    pull—


•


Use the Poisson equation to describe
the probability distribution
of random mutations in a cell that
affect ("hit") a particular gene ("target"):


•


Touch the eyelid closed with a damp finger—


•


$$P_x = \frac{b^x\, e^{-b}}{x!}$$


•


Playing Clue    counting her bean jars pinging—


•


*Rick's oaks died because they were all alike—*
chestnut blight, emerald ash bore, oak wilt,
Dutch elm disease, laminated root rot,
aspen canker, bacterial wetwood—


•


*The amount of fossil fuel required to cremate the North American
crop of bodies each year has been estimated to equal what an
automobile would use in more than eighty round trips to the moon.*


•

Good night *moon* good night *ACE inhibitors*

good night (to misquote myself) *farmhouse, fields*

good night *noises everywhere* good night *comb*—

•

One raven :: rearranging the meat—

•

I will do it—

*—row on thousands of rows* of yard-sale goods,
acres-to-let signs, falling-down silos.
The genetic modifications are
to enhance growth and durability.
The genetic modifications are
to enhance growth in corporate profits.
Here is your examination: Choose one.

Kernel :: cell :: syllable     I am her son

•

Use the swab     *sign here*     She is my mother

•

[*Hamartia*]

Poisons
the soil
to kill
the worm
that eats
the corn
that grows
in soil

•

So what's the *subject?*          water for the gums—

Meanwhile the haze air        and that calling pair

of doves farther apart        than you might suppose

flutes made of grasses        lower than her breath

until a jay cuts through      that scold that nag

on a moment's light           washing of breeze

yet all the trees blow        and simmer    above

which now many miles          across the village

the hot rods start up         guttural again

on a lit dust track           to see in a few

minutes which one may         cross over where

they all set off once         together    not now—

Untie the knots
        of your knuckles
    forgetting—

A short ride in the van, then
the eight of us there in the heat,

white shirtsleeves sticking, the women's
gloves off— fanning our faces.

The workers had set up
a big blue tent to help us at grave-

side tolerate the sun, which
was brutal all afternoon, as if

stationed above us, though it
edged limb to limb through

two huge covering elms—the long
processional of neighbors, friends,

the town's elderly, her beauty shop
familiars, her club's notables . . .

The world is full of prayers
arrived at from afterwards,

he said. Look up through the trees—
the leaves, curled there as

in self-control or quietly hurting
or now open, flat- palmed, many-

fine-veined,              and whether from
heat or sadness,          waving—

      •

Tell me your relation to pain, and I will tell you who you are!

      •

*I am looking   at trees   they may be one*
*of the things   I will miss   most from the earth*

she is my :: *cover her   when she sleeps*

Under English ivy

        the Bishop's weed

and its variegated

        soft sage blue-

and-teal each plant

        a labyrinthine mass

of roots so pulling

        up of one mandates

the pulling now of

        many, many-yards

long and under these

        the pachysandra

folded splayed but

        uncovered suddenly

to spring upright

        the lacelike tendril ferns

the hard starved-for-sun

        pale pathos of the

hostas the yard beneath

        my yard I find

as though beneath the

                    mind another mind—


            •


*But trees do not dwell only in the present. They remember the*
*past, and they anticipate the future. . . How trees remember, I*
*do not know. I have not been able to find out.*


            •


                    as under dogwoods ferns
as under mounds


                    of leaves and rank half
bales of straw a mass


                    of hanging baskets
trashed after our glad


                    seasons and shards of
terra cotta pots


                    soft-shouldered from
weathering and under


                    all of this the reeking
leaves and mulch become


                    rich loam again
I wheel it all barrow

                        by barrow to feed
the acrid hardpan

                        where the hungry
hollies the shallow-

                        rooted lilies of the
valley try to grow

                        I trowel it in    I
feed the earth the earth—

# FOUR

# Our Ivy

Star-gust. Seed cluster. Difficult syntax
of clouds through the yellow maple.
He flips
my paper to the porch these mornings
when he rises early to get his son
up, breakfasted, and driven off
to school.
It's *Hedera helix*—twisting ivy:
whose dark green, three-lobed leaves "grow alternate
along the stem" one by one and
waxy
as a living leather, who spreads ravenous
until it's covered the host tree's whole trunk
and thickens there, blossoms there, pre-
dator
or symbiotic partner, depending . . .

*We need to get that thing ripped out.* He means
the whole green mass. He rolls down his
window,
telling me as he slows into his drive.
But now he sees I've seen his face—*I'm fine,*
*more tests* . . . hairline where a doctor
shaved him
and four or five gauze bandage-spots dotting
his cheek and jaw. It's the actuary
in him—retired, insurance—
worried

about our cars, glass porches, passers-
by beneath the heavy shedding branches.
    Our ivy's in its jubilant
        phase, fall
    flower sunlight twisted through with shadow,

each bloom-cluster splayed along the lifting
    torso like a little nova
        outheld
    or geometric pincushion, eight, twelve,
sixteen spokes per globe with green-white blossoms
    —"if sufficient sunlight is avail-
        able"—
    which turn, come spring, into black berries and
"a few stony seeds." *I hate it.* He means
    the waiting now, the dark disease,
        coded
    in his gene swirl (from *melas* + *-oma*)
like a time bomb triggered by more sun.
    Our maple is beautiful, and
        dying,
    yellow leaves like flags, like pores, like patient

shaking wings, and the dark green, blunt, spearhead
    leaves of the ivy swirling in
        relief.
    One holds one up that pulls the other down.
I read somewhere the sky is blue because
    of Rayleigh scattering, shorter
        wavelength

atoms (blue, violet) absorbed and re-
distributed most readily. I've read
  the dust of long-blown stars seeds empty
    space.
  *Go get your saw*, he says. *I'll grab my gloves.*
About our ivy—I won't tell him—"new
  plants grow prolific from cuttings.
    They spread
  merely from stems making contact with earth."

# The Anniversary

All the years of nights

               rapt for each other

all the joy and later

               all the trouble

less trouble than joy

               and this one night's sky

so full of stars each

               flows farther away

as the low wing-wash

               of a hunting owl

so close over-

               head I didn't hear

until it was beyond

               all night walking

on the black road

               I didn't see pass

the great freighter

               of a shared life

furrows in the cut field

                              pushed up from a

prow I didn't know

                              had sailed by and

where has it gone—

# What You Said

But before I died I smelled them, I could
    have missed them so quickly *rushing elseward.*
Captivation depends don't you think on
    willingness sometimes to be caught be called
back as I was once, wet lowland where they
    were *Leucojum vernum* honey-like "They have
a slight fragrance" and a bright white button
    of blooms "as soon as the snow melts in its
wild habitat" or small pill-shaped pale
    with a green (occasionally yellow)
spot at the end of each tepal. Did you
    find them soothing, did you affiliate
—sane and sacred there—particularly
    in the singing, don't you think it's too late.
No I was walking for my health, lean down
    and savor there, heard *bleeding* the thrush *throat*
the lilac. You have gone too far you say
    things so as not to say something else. I
did wish to go back. Then you miss them
    —too early for lilac—tell me where's elseward—
I don't even know what were they snowdrops
    snowflakes *each to keep and all* and passed on
as quick as that, *you are everything that*
    *has not yet been lost* is what you said—

# The Quiet Side Street

1.

          where we live is lined

with dogwoods and maples
          with old man's beard

lined with many blue
          bins to recycle

things we cast away
          from us and gladly

that's how quiet
          you can hear crickets

a hundred feet above
          in a glister of

leaves leathery there
          with dew or brushed moon

bees mumbling at a
          hummingbird tube or

in spiked flowers of
          ivy crawling crazed

up the body of

each dying maple

when had you thought to

tell me    meanwhile

deer so still in the

folded woodruff

one hawk overhead

no one hears a thing

sometimes no one says

one thing until it's

too late here or there

we think we are fine

we are not as somewhere

in a room beneath

the clover meadow

a hand a joystick

guides the news    a drone

unmanned far away

or quietly above us

even now as we

call it homing in—

2.

He walks back from the     window in half-shadow

a half-shade himself     who first called them shades

who people the place     bereft of long life

he comes back he feels     with the fingers of one

hand the soft hem bed's     high edge to settle

back my father now     his bed his home or

we are walking now     he is walking carrying

me under starlight     under willows swept

with high wind crickets     two whippoorwills far

like two bells one bell     across the night hills

these long hills I am     so tired he thinks

I am sleeping who     peoples the night river

riffle of water here     over the newest stones

in the river all night     to the other side

okay he says at last or I say okay go

to sleep old man and when you waken on

the other side I'll be there we're there now

see our shadows where they have been waiting

as long as we've been here—

# Of Shine

What makes it
so—this "Shine
of Shining
things"? Not the
big dust-brick
mill turned gen-
trified condo
in the heart
of Olde Towne,
but new snow
pressed into

all its cupped
letters, RED
STAR BLANKETS,
which the sun
burns, blazes,
melting so
that the i-
cicles hanging
look now like
bright white veins
over the

very bones
of the building.
"Glory," said
the poet of

it, "made fine
To fill the
Fancy [get
this] peeping
through the Eyes
At thee." As,
don't look; as,

you'll be blind:
that's how wild
this shining
living is
that now "all
the wantons"
want to see,
small crowd decked
out in such
finery
as money

makes in these
gray parts, massed
across the
avenue
wet with slush,
craning up
where she in
her breasts and
he in his

best "flowing
flakes of bright-

est glories"
[it's in the
poem] trot
back and forth
before the
wide storage-
floor-turned-loft
window for
all the world
to see, "deckt
up in glory,"

thus.

# Two Iguanas

Spines in the
flame tree.
    And tongues beaded
    with blood just-drawn at the shuddering tip of

the two of them.
Males, if the expansive
    gullet, the ornate, fine-finned, armor-
    unfolding dewlap are

indicative, and the bigger jowl
and head
    are, too. One so big
    he straddles a flame bough, licking—tail drooping off

a good three feet.
He's been up there all the days we've been down here.
    Now the younger one—
    new-leaf-green along

his body and banded tail—
wants the cluster of
    flame blooms the big one
    was in the middle of

nipping off, chewing.
He's got

his whippy tail uplifted like
a bow, a scorpion.

All this time the tree seethes—
bone-brown boughs
    shine. Half a dozen doves and black grassquits
    sit up there and where

the red blossoms molder are a few
fern leaves and lime-like
    flower buds, buff as knuckles,
    growing in groupings.

I think the big one
sees the little one, though he's below—
    perhaps the rudiment of lens and retina in
    the flat third eye

senses motion. They're hardly moving,
except for the talon claws
    of the big one twitching at
    the limb, the slow-

motion, pushup
tensing of the small one like
    a breeze, itself sweet
    with a tincture of hunger and heady scent

of a hundred hibiscus and
pink cedar flowers.
    Then he falls!—or
    did he just jump, the big one?—forty feet down in

a crashing now of vines
and brittle limbs . . . and hits the
    ground hard, with a thump, and lifts to look back
    through the canopy.

He's been up there all our days.

And now he's going up again.

# Heaven

All afternoon the sprinkler ticks and sprays,
ticks and sprays in lazy rounds, trailing
a feather of mist. When I turn it off,
the cicadas keep up their own dry rain,
passing on high from limb to limb.

I don't know what has shocked me more,
that you are gone, that I am still here,
that there is music after the end.

# Metastasis

Then the breakers turning back to brightness, if the light's
    opaque ocean-blue sameness in the sky can be said to break,
the way the waves themselves, blue in back of blue
    like a color in the eye, fall back to the wall, sea wrack,
driftwood, or the inner optic shelf behind the lens.
Then the gulls and simple cirrus strands turn back to light.
Then to inland sparrows, drifting under blue Ohio's sky—
    it's a work day, and the heat is the heat of the color
of your clothes, wash day, and hands hurt from swinging of a scythe.
Then it's day into night at the heart of the seeds
that fell from your hands breaking open, strewn in rows
    like water along the ancient seabed floor of the farm.
Someone is standing at the door. Someone is waving from the car.
    This day and that one sinking to brightness and the blue
evening wall before that, like a spark that fell from the star
    becoming, as you will say, one day, all we will become.

# NOTES

A poem lives among poems. In addition to quotations I've attributed in these poems—for instance to Emily Dickinson and John Clare—I have picked among other poets and writers, reusing phrases of theirs among mine, including John Berryman, Stacey D'Erasmo, Robert Hass, Joanna Klink, Dana Levin, W. S. Merwin, Stanley Plumly, Theodore Roethke, Mary Ruefle, Mark Strand, Edward Taylor, Wang Wei, Dara Weir, Walt Whitman, and Franz Wright.

These poems are dedicated to the following people: "What Is a Weed?" to Katie Baker; "Scavenger Loop" to Martha Baker *in memoriam*; "Two Iguanas" to Page Hill Starzinger.

### "Five Odes on Absence"

Among John Clare's late letters, written during his long residency at the Northampton General Lunatic Asylum, was a draft of a letter to a Mary Collingwood. Like a few others, this letter was written in Clare's code—an erasure of vowels and the letter *y*. Jonathan Bate reckons that Clare may have used code to protect his privacy in case someone was going through his notebooks. Or, Bate continues, "the disappearance of the vowels may have been a step on the road to the later mental degeneration that led him to speak of how his head had been cut off."

My poem includes the following phrases from Clare's letter. After each phrase I present here its likely meaning: *M Drst . . . M nrl wrn t* / My Dearest . . . I am nearly worn out. *Nbd wll wn M r hv m . . . & wht hv dn . . .* / Nobody will own (want?) me or have me . . . and what have I done. *ppl tll m hv gt n hm n ths wrld . . .* / People tell me I have got no home in this world. *Drst Mr r fthfll r d thnk f m . . . dd vst me n hll sm tm bck . . . flsh ppl tll m hv gt n hm n ths wrld . . .* / Dearest Mary are you faithful or do you think of me . . . you did visit me in hell sometime back . . . foolish people tell me I have got no home in this world. *whr r th* / Where are they? *bt dnt cm hr gn fr t s ntrs bd plc . . . rs fr vr & vr Jhn Clr* / But don't come here again for it is a notorious bad place . . . yours for ever and ever John Clare.

I reprint several lines from a manuscript draft of Clare's long poem, "October," part of his *The Shepherd's Calendar*. The cross-outs and revisions are Clare's.

### "Scavenger Loop"

I have rummaged through many other writers' works to compose this sequence. Among those I directly quote or cite are Bernd Heinrich (*Life Everlasting*), Melanie Challenger (*On Extinction*), Frederick Seidel ("Green Absinthe"), Monsanto Corporation (online product information), Ron Sterk ("Crunch Time for Midwest Corn Growers"), Richard Conniff ("What Are Species Worth?"), Louise Glück ("First Snow"), Edward Taylor ("Meditation 49"), Mario Santiago Papasquiaro ("Advice from 1 Disciple of Marx to 1 Heidegger Fanatic"), Gerard Manley Hopkins ("The Starlight Night"), Margaret Wise Brown (*Goodnight Moon*), W. S. Merwin ("Elegy," "Words from a Totem Animal," "Trees"), Ernst Jünger (*On Pain*), Brenda Hillman ("Light Galaxies Sleep for Our Mother"), Colin Tudge (*The Tree*), and Nick Reding (*Methland*). I have referred to sites provided by the American Medical Association, the United States Department of Agriculture, and both Wikipedia and Facebook. A few lines and passages from my own previous work are woven into this sequence, having first appeared in the *Connecticut Review*, *Five Points*, *Hotel Amerika*, *Literary Imagination*, and the *Virginia Quarterly Review*.